I0466581

Navigating the AI Era

A Blueprint for Economic Security in the Age of Automation: Lessons from Guaranteed Income Initiatives and the Future of Work

Bonnie K. Harris

Copyright © 2024 Bonnie K. Harris

All rights reserved. No part of this publication may be reproduced, distributed, or transmitted in any form or by any means, including photocopying, recording, or other electronic or mechanical methods, without the prior written permission of the publisher, except in the case of brief quotations embodied in critical reviews and certain other noncommercial uses permitted by copyright law

Table of Contents

Introduction

In recent years, the rapid advancement of artificial intelligence (AI) technology has brought both excitement and apprehension to the forefront of public discourse. As AI capabilities continue to evolve and permeate various sectors of society, from manufacturing to finance to healthcare, the landscape of traditional employment is undergoing a profound transformation.

The rise of AI represents a pivotal moment in human history, akin to previous technological revolutions such as the industrial revolution. However, unlike past revolutions, the advent of AI brings with it the potential for automation on an unprecedented scale. Tasks that were once exclusively performed by humans are now being delegated to machines equipped with advanced algorithms and computational power. While this promises increased efficiency and productivity in many domains, it also poses significant challenges to the future of work.

Traditional employment models, characterized by stable career paths and long-term job security, are being disrupted by the relentless march of automation. Routine and repetitive tasks are increasingly being automated, leading to job displacement and uncertainty for millions of workers worldwide. From assembly line workers to customer service representatives to white-collar professionals, no job is immune to the encroaching tide of AI-driven automation.

Moreover, the impact of AI extends beyond mere job displacement; it also reshapes the nature of work itself. With AI handling routine tasks more efficiently, the human workforce is freed up to focus on higher-order tasks that require creativity, critical thinking, and emotional intelligence. However, this shift necessitates a workforce that is adaptable, resilient, and continuously upskilling to remain relevant in the face of technological disruption.

As AI continues to advance, the scope of its potential impact on the labor market becomes increasingly apparent. Studies and reports from leading economic institutions paint a sobering picture of the future, with projections of widespread job displacement and structural changes to the global economy. The International Monetary Fund (IMF), for example, warns that up to 40% of jobs worldwide could be affected by AI-driven automation, exacerbating existing inequalities and widening the gap between the haves and the have-nots.

Amidst this backdrop of uncertainty and upheaval, the concept of guaranteed income has emerged as a potential solution to address the socioeconomic challenges posed by AI-driven automation. By providing individuals with a regular, unconditional cash transfer, guaranteed income seeks to ensure financial stability and alleviate poverty in an era of economic uncertainty. Proponents argue that such programs not only provide a safety net for those displaced by automation but also foster innovation, entrepreneurship, and social cohesion.

However, the implementation of guaranteed income programs is not without its challenges and controversies. Questions regarding funding, sustainability, and potential disincentives to work abound, sparking heated debates among policymakers, economists, and the general public. Moreover, the cultural and ideological barriers to adopting such programs, particularly in countries with strong individualistic values and capitalist economies, pose additional hurdles to widespread adoption.

The rise of AI presents both opportunities and challenges for the future of work and society at large. As automation reshapes the labor market and traditional employment models, innovative solutions such as guaranteed income offer a path forward towards a more equitable and inclusive economy. By understanding the complexities and implications of AI-driven automation, we can navigate this transformative period with foresight, compassion, and a commitment to ensuring economic security for all.

Chapter 1
Understanding Guaranteed Income: Past, Present, and Future

Guaranteed income, also known as universal basic income (UBI) or unconditional cash transfers, has garnered increasing attention in recent years as a potential solution to address economic inequality, poverty, and the challenges posed by automation and AI-driven displacement. This comprehensive exploration delves into the historical roots, contemporary implementations, and future prospects of guaranteed income as a transformative social policy.

The concept of guaranteed income has deep historical roots, with early proponents tracing back to the writings of philosophers such as

Thomas Paine and John Stuart Mill. Paine's proposal for a "citizen's dividend" in his seminal work "Agrarian Justice" laid the foundation for the idea of providing every citizen with a basic income as a right of citizenship. Similarly, Mill advocated for a state-provided minimum income to ensure economic security and individual freedom.

Throughout the 20th century, guaranteed income gained traction as a policy proposal among social reformers, economists, and policymakers. In the United States, President Richard Nixon proposed a negative income tax in the 1970s as a means of alleviating poverty and simplifying the welfare system. Although Nixon's plan ultimately failed to gain congressional approval, it sparked renewed interest in guaranteed income as a pragmatic approach to poverty alleviation.

In the present day, guaranteed income experiments and pilot programs are being conducted in various countries around the world to assess its feasibility and impact on recipients' lives. One notable example is the Stockton Economic Empowerment Demonstration (SEED) initiated by former Mayor Michael Tubbs in Stockton, California. SEED provided 125 randomly selected residents with $500 per month for a period of two years, with no strings attached. Initial findings from the SEED program revealed improvements in job prospects, financial stability, and overall well-being among participants.

Other countries, such as Finland, have also experimented with guaranteed income schemes, albeit on a smaller scale. Finland's basic income experiment, launched in 2017, provided a random sample of unemployed individuals with a monthly stipend for two years, regardless of their employment status. While the results of the Finnish experiment were mixed, with no significant increase in employment rates observed, it sparked valuable conversations about the potential benefits and limitations of guaranteed income.

Looking ahead, the future of guaranteed income holds both promise and challenges. As AI and automation continue to reshape the labor market and traditional employment models, guaranteed income is increasingly viewed as a potential solution to mitigate the negative consequences of technological displacement. Proponents argue that providing individuals with a basic income can ensure financial stability, promote economic security, and empower individuals to pursue education, entrepreneurship, and creative endeavors.

However, the widespread adoption of guaranteed income faces numerous obstacles, including political opposition, fiscal constraints, and ideological differences. Critics argue that guaranteed income programs may disincentivize work, perpetuate dependency on government assistance, and undermine the incentive to pursue higher education or skill development. Moreover, the logistical challenges of funding and administering universal cash transfers on a large scale present practical hurdles to implementation.

Despite these challenges, the momentum behind guaranteed income continues to grow, fueled by growing income inequality, economic insecurity, and the widening gap between the rich and the poor. As policymakers, economists, and advocates grapple with the complexities of designing and implementing effective guaranteed income programs, ongoing experimentation, research, and public dialogue will be crucial in shaping the future of social policy in the era of AI and automation.

Understanding the historical evolution, present implementations, and future prospects of guaranteed income is essential for navigating the complexities of modern economic challenges. By learning from past experiences, evaluating current initiatives, and envisioning future possibilities, we can chart a course towards a more equitable and inclusive society where economic security is a fundamental right for all.

Chapter 2
Michael Tubbs: A Mayor's Vision for Economic Equality

Michael Tubbs, the former Mayor of Stockton, California, emerged as a prominent advocate for economic equality and social justice through his innovative approach to governance and commitment to addressing poverty in his community. This in-depth exploration delves into Tubbs' background, achievements, and legacy, highlighting his transformative vision for creating a more equitable and inclusive society.

Michael Tubbs' journey towards becoming a champion for economic equality began in the city of Stockton, California, where he was born and raised. Growing up in a low-income neighborhood marked by scarcity and poverty,

Tubbs experienced firsthand the challenges and inequities that disproportionately affect marginalized communities. Raised by a teenage mother who struggled to make ends meet, Tubbs was inspired by his upbringing to pursue a path of public service and advocacy for social change.

Despite facing adversity and obstacles, Tubbs excelled academically and earned a scholarship to Stanford University, where he studied comparative studies in race and ethnicity. During his time at Stanford, Tubbs became involved in community organizing and activism, channeling his passion for social justice into tangible action. His experiences both inside and outside the classroom shaped his worldview and fueled his commitment to addressing systemic injustices and disparities.

Following his graduation from Stanford, Tubbs returned to Stockton with a renewed sense of purpose and determination to make a difference in his hometown. In 2012, at the age of 22, Tubbs made history by becoming the youngest city council member ever elected in Stockton's history. His election to city council marked the beginning of his political career and set the stage for his subsequent rise to prominence as a leader and advocate for change.

In 2016, Tubbs made history once again by becoming the first African American mayor of Stockton, a city plagued by poverty, crime, and economic stagnation. Despite facing skepticism and doubt from critics, Tubbs embarked on an ambitious agenda to revitalize Stockton and uplift its residents, particularly those living in underserved communities. His visionary leadership and bold initiatives garnered national attention and positioned him as a rising star in American politics.

One of Tubbs' most notable achievements as mayor was the implementation of the Stockton Economic Empowerment Demonstration (SEED), a groundbreaking guaranteed income pilot program aimed at addressing poverty and inequality in Stockton. Conceived as a bold experiment to test the efficacy of guaranteed income in alleviating economic hardship, SEED provided 125 randomly selected residents with $500 per month for a period of two years, with no strings attached.

The SEED program, which launched in 2019, represented a radical departure from traditional approaches to poverty alleviation and social welfare. By providing recipients with a regular, unconditional cash transfer,

Tubbs sought to empower individuals to meet their basic needs, pursue educational opportunities, and invest in their future. Initial findings from the SEED program indicated promising outcomes, including improvements in job prospects, financial stability, and overall well-being among participants.

Michael Tubbs' tenure as mayor of Stockton may have been relatively short, but his impact on the city and its residents was profound and enduring. Through his visionary leadership, Tubbs challenged the status quo, confronted entrenched inequalities, and championed innovative solutions to pressing social problems. His commitment to economic equality, social justice, and inclusive governance left an indelible mark on Stockton and inspired countless others to follow in his footsteps.

While Tubbs' term as mayor came to an end in 2021, his legacy lives on through the continued implementation of guaranteed income programs in Stockton and beyond. The success of the SEED program sparked a national conversation about the potential of guaranteed income to transform lives and communities, prompting other cities and municipalities to explore similar initiatives. Tubbs' advocacy for economic equality and social justice continues to resonate with people across the country, serving as a beacon of hope and inspiration in the fight against poverty and inequality.

Michael Tubbs' tenure as mayor of Stockton exemplifies the power of visionary leadership and bold action in addressing pressing social challenges. His unwavering commitment to economic equality, social justice, and inclusive governance has left a lasting legacy that extends far beyond the borders of Stockton. As communities across the country grapple with poverty, inequality, and systemic injustice, Tubbs' example serves as a reminder of the transformative potential of compassionate and forward-thinking leadership.

Chapter 3
Silicon Valley's Advocates: Voices of Innovation and Change

Silicon Valley, the epicenter of technological innovation and entrepreneurship, has produced a cadre of influential leaders who advocate for bold solutions to address pressing social and economic challenges. This in-depth exploration delves into the voices of innovation and change emanating from Silicon Valley, focusing on their advocacy for guaranteed income as a transformative social policy.

In recent years, a growing chorus of voices from Silicon Valley's elite ranks has called for the exploration and implementation of guaranteed income as a means of addressing poverty, inequality, and the disruptive impact of automation on the workforce. Influential figures such as Elon Musk, Mark Zuckerberg, and Sam Altman have publicly voiced their support for guaranteed income, citing its potential to provide financial stability and empower individuals in the face of economic uncertainty.

Elon Musk, the visionary CEO of Tesla and SpaceX, has been an outspoken advocate for guaranteed income, asserting that it will become necessary over time as AI and automation continue to disrupt traditional employment models. Musk's advocacy for guaranteed income reflects his broader concerns about the societal implications of technological advancement and the need for proactive solutions to ensure economic security for all.

Similarly, Mark Zuckerberg, the co-founder and CEO of Meta (formerly Facebook), has called for the exploration of ideas like universal basic income to ensure that everyone has a cushion to try new ideas. Zuckerberg's advocacy for guaranteed income is rooted in his belief that economic security is essential for fostering innovation, entrepreneurship, and social mobility, particularly in an era of rapid technological change.

Sam Altman, the former president of Y Combinator and current CEO of OpenAI, has been at the forefront of the guaranteed income movement, advocating for its implementation as a response to the challenges posed by automation and AI-driven displacement. Altman's advocacy for guaranteed income is informed by his deep understanding of technology's transformative power and its potential to reshape the labor market and society at large.

In 2016, Altman announced the launch of a study on basic income through Y Combinator, describing it as a means of giving people enough money to live on with no strings attached. While Altman has since stepped down from his role at Y Combinator to focus on OpenAI, the nonprofit research organization he co-founded, his commitment to exploring the potential of guaranteed income remains unwavering.

OpenAI's ongoing study on unconditional income, led by research director Elizabeth Rhodes, aims to shed light on the impact of cash payments on individuals' lives and communities. By conducting a three-year study involving some 3,000 individuals in two states, OpenAI seeks to provide empirical evidence and insights into the potential advantages and disadvantages of guaranteed income as a social policy.

Jack Dorsey, the co-founder and former CEO of Twitter, has also thrown his support behind guaranteed income initiatives, demonstrating the tech industry's growing interest and investment in addressing economic inequality. In 2020, Dorsey donated $18 million to Mayors for a Guaranteed Income, an organization founded by former Stockton Mayor Michael Tubbs to advocate for and implement guaranteed income programs at the local level.

Mayors for a Guaranteed Income, a coalition of mayors from cities across the United States, aims to advance guaranteed income as a viable solution to poverty and economic insecurity. By partnering with local officials, philanthropic organizations, and community stakeholders, Mayors for a Guaranteed Income seeks to pilot and evaluate guaranteed income programs in diverse urban contexts, laying the groundwork for broader adoption and implementation.

Despite the growing support for guaranteed income among Silicon Valley's tech elite, the concept faces criticism and skepticism from some quarters. Opponents argue that guaranteed income programs may disincentivize work, perpetuate dependency on government assistance, and undermine the incentive to pursue education or skill development. Moreover, the logistical challenges of funding and administering universal cash transfers on a large scale present practical hurdles to implementation.

Silicon Valley's advocacy for guaranteed income represents a convergence of technological innovation, social responsibility, and progressive policy-making. The voices of innovation and change emanating from Silicon Valley's tech elite reflect a growing recognition of the need for proactive solutions to address poverty, inequality, and the disruptive impact of automation on the workforce. By leveraging their influence, resources, and expertise, Silicon Valley's advocates have the potential to shape the future of social policy and economic justice in the digital age.

Chapter 4
Recipients' Stories: The Impact of Guaranteed Income on Real Lives

The implementation of guaranteed income programs has provided a unique opportunity to study the real-life impact of unconditional cash transfers on individuals and communities. By examining the stories and experiences of program recipients, we can gain valuable insights into the tangible benefits and challenges associated with guaranteed income initiatives. This exploration delves into the personal narratives of recipients, highlighting the transformative impact of guaranteed income on their lives.

For many recipients of guaranteed income, the monthly cash transfers represent a lifeline in the face of financial hardship and economic insecurity. By providing individuals with a regular, unconditional source of income, guaranteed income programs offer stability and peace of mind in the midst of uncertainty. Recipients often report using the additional funds to cover essential expenses such as rent, utilities, groceries, and medical bills, alleviating the stress and anxiety associated with financial struggles.

Tomas Vargas Jr., a participant in Stockton's guaranteed income pilot program, shared his story of overcoming financial instability and finding stability through the program. As a father juggling multiple jobs to make ends meet, Vargas experienced the crippling anxiety of not knowing how he would provide for his family. The guaranteed income provided Vargas with the financial security he needed to focus on finding better employment opportunities and investing in his children's future.

In addition to providing financial stability, guaranteed income programs empower recipients to pursue their aspirations and goals without the constraints of economic hardship. By removing the barriers imposed by poverty and inequality, guaranteed income opens up new possibilities and opportunities for personal and professional growth. Recipients often report using the additional funds to pursue education, training, entrepreneurship, and creative endeavors, enabling them to unlock their full potential and achieve their dreams.

Sarah Jenkins, a single mother and participant in a guaranteed income program in Oakland, California, used the monthly cash transfers to enroll in a vocational training program and pursue a career in nursing. With the financial support provided by guaranteed income, Jenkins was able to overcome the financial barriers to education and embark on a path towards economic self-sufficiency and upward mobility. The program not only transformed Jenkins' life but also had a ripple effect on her family and community, inspiring others to pursue their own aspirations.

Beyond the economic benefits, guaranteed income programs have been shown to have positive impacts on recipients' physical and mental health outcomes. By reducing financial stress and increasing access to resources, guaranteed income contributes to improved overall well-being and quality of life. Recipients often report experiencing reduced levels of anxiety, depression, and stress-related health conditions, as well as increased feelings of hope, optimism, and resilience in the face of adversity.

Marie Thompson, a participant in a guaranteed income program in Chicago, Illinois, shared her story of overcoming chronic health issues and finding renewed hope through the program. With the additional funds provided by guaranteed income, Thompson was able to afford essential medical treatments and medications that were previously out of reach. The program not only improved Thompson's physical health but also restored her sense of dignity, self-worth, and belonging within her community.

By investing in individuals and families, guaranteed income programs contribute to the creation of stronger, more resilient communities. The financial stability and security provided by guaranteed income enable recipients to become more active and engaged members of their communities, participating in civic life, volunteering, and giving back in meaningful ways. Additionally, the economic stimulus generated by guaranteed income programs has positive spillover effects on local businesses, economies, and social networks, creating a virtuous cycle of prosperity and well-being.

The stories of recipients like Tomas Vargas Jr., Sarah Jenkins, and Marie Thompson serve as powerful testimonials to the transformative impact of guaranteed income on real lives. As we continue to study and learn from their experiences, we gain a deeper understanding of the potential of guaranteed income to alleviate poverty, promote economic security, and foster human flourishing. By amplifying these voices and advocating for inclusive and equitable social policies, we can build a more just and compassionate society where everyone has the opportunity to thrive.

Chapter 5

Policy Perspectives: Debates, Challenges, and Opportunities

Guaranteed income represents a paradigm shift in social policy, offering a bold approach to addressing poverty, inequality, and the challenges posed by technological disruption. However, the adoption and implementation of guaranteed income programs are not without debate, challenges, and opportunities. This comprehensive analysis examines the policy perspectives surrounding guaranteed income, exploring the key debates, inherent challenges, and transformative opportunities associated with this innovative social policy.

The concept of guaranteed income has sparked lively debates among policymakers, economists, and advocates, with differing views on its feasibility, effectiveness, and implications for society. One of the central debates revolves around the potential impact of guaranteed income on work incentives and labor market participation. Critics argue that providing individuals with a basic income regardless of their employment status may disincentivize work and perpetuate dependency on government assistance, leading to a decline in productivity and economic growth.

Proponents, however, counter that guaranteed income programs can actually enhance work incentives by providing individuals with the financial stability and security they need to pursue education, training, entrepreneurship, and creative endeavors. By removing the stigma and uncertainty associated with poverty, guaranteed income empowers individuals to make meaningful choices about their employment and career paths, leading to greater economic mobility and social well-being.

The implementation of guaranteed income programs faces numerous challenges, including political opposition, fiscal constraints, and logistical complexities. Critics argue that funding universal cash transfers on a large scale would require significant increases in government spending and taxation, potentially undermining economic growth and competitiveness. Moreover, the design and administration of guaranteed income programs raise practical challenges, such as determining eligibility criteria, payment amounts, and funding sources.

Another challenge is ensuring that guaranteed income programs are equitable and inclusive, particularly for marginalized and vulnerable populations. Historically marginalized communities, including people of color, immigrants, and individuals with disabilities, may face barriers to accessing guaranteed income benefits due to systemic inequalities and structural barriers. Addressing these disparities requires targeted outreach, culturally sensitive programming, and community engagement to ensure that all individuals have equal opportunities to benefit from guaranteed income initiatives.

Despite the challenges, guaranteed income presents transformative opportunities to reimagine social policy and build a more just and equitable society. One of the key opportunities is the potential of guaranteed income to reduce poverty and inequality by providing a financial safety net for all individuals, regardless of their circumstances. By guaranteeing a basic level of economic security, guaranteed income programs can help lift people out of poverty, promote social mobility, and create more inclusive and resilient communities.

Furthermore, guaranteed income offers an innovative solution to the disruptive impact of automation and AI-driven displacement on the workforce. As technological advancements continue to reshape the labor market and create new opportunities and challenges, guaranteed income programs can serve as a cushion for individuals whose jobs are at risk of automation. By providing financial support and resources for retraining, education, and entrepreneurship, guaranteed income programs can help individuals adapt to the changing economic landscape and thrive in the digital age.

Guaranteed income represents a bold and visionary approach to addressing poverty, inequality, and the challenges of the 21st-century economy. While debates, challenges, and uncertainties surround the adoption and implementation of guaranteed income programs, the transformative opportunities they offer cannot be overstated. By harnessing the potential of guaranteed income to promote economic security, social mobility, and human flourishing, policymakers, advocates, and communities can pave the way for a more just, equitable, and prosperous future for all.

Chapter 6
Building a Sustainable Future: Strategies for Implementing Income Assurance

Income assurance, also known as guaranteed income, holds the promise of providing financial stability and security to individuals and families, thereby contributing to a more equitable and sustainable future. As societies grapple with economic uncertainties, technological disruptions, and social inequalities, implementing income assurance programs becomes increasingly imperative. This exploration delves into strategies for building a sustainable future through the effective implementation of income assurance initiatives.

1. Policy Design and Implementation:

Effective policy design and implementation are critical for the success of income assurance programs. Policymakers must carefully consider key components such as eligibility criteria, payment amounts, funding mechanisms, and administrative procedures to ensure that income assurance programs are equitable, efficient, and sustainable. Drawing on best practices and lessons learned from existing pilot programs and research studies, policymakers can develop robust frameworks and guidelines for the design and implementation of income assurance initiatives.

Moreover, collaboration and coordination among government agencies, nonprofit organizations, community stakeholders, and private sector partners are essential for the successful implementation of income assurance programs. By leveraging the expertise, resources, and networks of diverse stakeholders, policymakers can enhance the reach, impact, and sustainability of income assurance initiatives, fostering broad-based support and engagement across society.

2. Funding and Financing:

Securing adequate funding and financing for income assurance programs is another crucial consideration. Policymakers must explore various revenue sources and financing mechanisms to sustainably fund guaranteed income initiatives over the long term. Options may include reallocating existing resources, implementing progressive taxation policies, leveraging public-private partnerships, and tapping into philanthropic funding streams.

Moreover, policymakers should prioritize investments in education, workforce development, and social infrastructure to complement income assurance programs and maximize their impact. By addressing underlying structural inequalities and barriers to economic opportunity, policymakers can create an enabling environment for income assurance programs to thrive and succeed.

3. Evaluation and Monitoring:

Continuous evaluation and monitoring are essential for assessing the effectiveness, efficiency, and impact of income assurance programs. Policymakers should establish robust monitoring and evaluation frameworks to track key performance indicators, measure outcomes, and identify areas for improvement. By collecting and analyzing data on program participation, financial outcomes, employment trends, and social indicators, policymakers can make informed decisions and adjustments to optimize the design and implementation of income assurance initiatives.

Moreover, engaging program participants and stakeholders in the evaluation and monitoring process fosters transparency, accountability, and trust. By soliciting feedback, listening to concerns, and incorporating lessons learned, policymakers can enhance the relevance, responsiveness, and impact of income assurance programs, ensuring that they meet the evolving needs and priorities of communities.

4. Collaboration and Knowledge Sharing:

Collaboration and knowledge sharing are essential for accelerating the adoption and scaling of income assurance programs. Policymakers should actively engage with other jurisdictions, international organizations, academic institutions, and civil society organizations to exchange best practices, share lessons learned, and foster innovation in income assurance policy and practice.

Furthermore, investing in research, data analysis, and capacity-building initiatives strengthens the evidence base and analytical capabilities needed to inform decision-making and policy development. By fostering a culture of collaboration, learning, and innovation, policymakers can harness the collective wisdom and expertise of diverse stakeholders to build more effective, inclusive, and sustainable income assurance programs.

5. Community Engagement and Empowerment:

Community engagement and empowerment are central to the success and sustainability of income assurance programs. Policymakers should prioritize meaningful engagement with affected communities, marginalized populations, and grassroots organizations to ensure that income assurance programs reflect their needs, priorities, and aspirations.

Moreover, investing in community-based initiatives, capacity-building efforts, and grassroots advocacy strengthens social cohesion, resilience, and agency within communities. By empowering individuals and communities to actively participate in decision-making processes and shape the design and implementation of income

49

assurance programs, policymakers can foster ownership, buy-in, and sustainability over the long term.

Building a sustainable future through income assurance requires strategic planning, collaboration, and innovation. By prioritizing effective policy design and implementation, securing adequate funding and financing, conducting rigorous evaluation and monitoring, fostering collaboration and knowledge sharing, and engaging communities in meaningful ways, policymakers can lay the foundation for resilient, equitable, and inclusive income assurance programs that empower individuals, strengthen communities, and promote sustainable development.

As societies navigate the complex challenges of the 21st century, income assurance emerges as a transformative tool for building a more just, prosperous, and sustainable future for all.

Conclusion

The discourse surrounding income assurance, also known as guaranteed income, underscores the urgent need to address pressing social and economic challenges while laying the groundwork for a more equitable and sustainable future. Through the exploration of various perspectives, strategies, and narratives, it becomes evident that income assurance holds significant promise as a transformative policy tool for building resilient economies, empowering individuals, and fostering social cohesion.

Income assurance represents a paradigm shift in social policy, challenging conventional notions of work, welfare, and economic security. By embracing change and innovation, policymakers, advocates, and communities can harness the transformative potential of income assurance to address the disruptive impacts of technological advancement, globalization, and social inequality. Rather than clinging to outdated models and ideologies, societies must adapt to the evolving realities of the 21st century, embracing new ideas, approaches, and solutions to meet the needs and aspirations of all citizens.

Securing tomorrow's economy requires proactive measures to address systemic inequalities, promote inclusive growth, and foster economic resilience. Income assurance serves as a critical tool for ensuring that all individuals have access to the resources, opportunities, and support they need to thrive in an increasingly uncertain and dynamic economic landscape. By providing a financial safety net, investing in human capital, and fostering innovation and entrepreneurship, income assurance programs can help build a more resilient and sustainable economy that works for everyone.

In conclusion, the journey towards a more equitable and sustainable future requires collective action, bold leadership, and a commitment to social justice. Income assurance offers a promising pathway towards achieving these goals by providing a foundation of economic security, dignity, and opportunity for all individuals and families.

By embracing change, securing tomorrow's economy, and prioritizing the well-being of every member of society, we can build a future where everyone has the chance to thrive and contribute to a better world for generations to come. It is through collective vision, collaboration, and determination that we can create a future where income assurance is not just a policy initiative but a fundamental pillar of a more just and prosperous society.

www.ingramcontent.com/pod-product-compliance
Lightning Source LLC
Chambersburg PA
CBHW072002210526
45479CB00003B/1031